Hear THE
RIVER DAMMED

Poems from the Edge of the Mississippi

COLE W. WILLIAMS

Edited by Hanna Kjeldbjerg
Cover art by Ann Aubitz

ISBN 13: 978-1-59298-807-5
Library of Congress Catalog Number: 2017904301
Printed in the United States of America
First Printing: 2017
21 20 19 18 17   5 4 3 2 1

BEAVER'S
POND
PRESS

Beaver's Pond Press
7108 Ohms Lane
Edina, MN 55439–2129
(952) 829-8818
www.BeaversPondPress.com

To order, visit www.colewwilliams.com
Reseller discounts available.

Printed in the United States of America.

Contents

Acknowledgments

To the River, an inspiring, meandering giant in the backyard of the Twin Cities. It quietly beckons us to lean in and learn. I look forward to many more years of discovery with the great Mississippi River.

To the writing communities, to the artists, and to the water protectors.

To the scrupulous editor, proofreaders, and family cheerleaders. I am loath to edit my own work and rely heavily on these keen eagle eyes.

To the freedom of independence in publishing, and the places that take a chance on us.

To my husband for being my number-one supporter, always the first to read and pontificate upon each poem with me. These poems are an homage to the life we build.

Coda: Teach the Children

Our first home is water.
How grateful they are,
picnics at the beach,
sand in sandwiches,
toes at the water's edge.
Then knees, waist, heart, hair,
eyes open in wavering light.

—James P. Lenfestey

River Musings

When I first told people my family was moving into a home on the Mississippi River, I was greeted with an assortment of antipathy and confused looks. The usual responses would entail musings such as, "Ew, that river is so gross! Do you swim in it?" or, "You know what they did to that river, right? You don't eat fish from there, do you?"

These queries left me slow to respond with something salient enough to sway the misconceptions. Partially because I myself did not know if these claims carried legitimacy. But I wanted to know. I wanted to supply them with an introspective answer that was fair and inspiring.

I believe we should never lose the curiosity of a child, the traveler (even if only exploring our own backyards), or the scientist. How easily this sense of wonder is forgotten as we age. As adults, as moderns, we have to be careful of losing that which makes us animal. We've not yet evolved from our need to be enmeshed with the natural environment; it makes us whole, happy, and healthy.

This loss of connection may very well be a new plague in modern society. As Bryan Pfeiffer wrote in "Ghosts and Tiny Treasures" for *Aeon*, inspired by his tenacious searches for the ivory-billed woodpecker:

*Now, seated before the glowing screen, we whip and
zoom with white-throated swifts along the course of the
Colorado River through the Grand Canyon, we migrate
with wildebeasts across the Serengeti, we swim among
coral and dolphins at the Great Barrier Reef. Never
have we been so figuratively close to wildlife—and yet
so far. Our gadgets and electronic maps read our exact
location and desires virtually anytime and anywhere.
Never before have we been so located—and yet so lost.*

I decided to get to know this river.

I started simply.

Learn with me. What is a watershed? Taken directly from
the South Washington Watershed District website: "A watershed
is all the land area that drains to a specific water resource,
such as a lake or stream. Watersheds range in size from a few
square miles to an entire continent. They provide water for
drinking, irrigation . . . fishing, swimming and boating." (For
more information, visit http://www.swwdmn.org/about.)

Honestly, this didn't connect with me in a mind-to-hands sort
of way until a volunteer stint with the Friends of the Mississippi
River one evening. We were tasked with spray-painting sewer
drains, handing out conservation material, and cleaning up
garbage in downtown St. Paul. I was excited thinking about the
microbrew afterwards, when I started to have an epiphany of
sorts—every little cigarette butt and radiator leak is *also part of
our watershed.*

I imagined the profound extrapolation of what we picked
up that day off the ground compared to what was left for the
drains. It's important to understand the watershed concept
and to investigate the one you both utilize for your water *and*

contribute to. Starting simply like that is okay, because it's the connection many of us urgently need to find again. Everyone I spoke to on that afternoon of volunteering was eager to learn about what they could do. People want to help.

As the river water thaws each spring and we see the current start to emerge, my family witnesses, from our backyard, a great garbage dump. The pier becomes lined with bag after bag of what the upper river has donated to us. We take the time to sort the garbage from recyclable materials. Plastic bottles are the most obvious harvest of this task. I adopted a River Mile through Living Lands & Waters, and it is now "part of the family." This process has begun to come naturally to us. But how do we prevent this before it begins?

Take a day or two a year to help clean up a corner of the river or commit to using a reusable beverage container. Ask your favorite coffee dive to offer incentives for those who bring in their own mug. On a smaller scale, and hidden from the naked eye, are the effects of chemicals and runoff that infiltrate the river. Look into the countless ways your family can reduce pressure on your watershed and help keep the river clean, www.cleanwatermn.org offers homeowner tips and check out the resource section at the back of this book for more ideas on how to take action with your local river mile.

A true and lasting love grows with deeper understanding and patience. I continued on.

We made the most of our summer on the river and discovered a robust river community, seemingly clandestine from its close proximity to city life. It was unbeknownst to most people that this oasis was right behind a nearby tree line—camping, fishing, and swimming from bank to bank, especially as you near Hastings. I learned that the section of river I've spent much of my life on—skipping rocks at the Minnehaha Falls dog park, cruising down during the Minneapolis Aquatennial fireworks, and hedging my bets in the morning commutes—also happens to be the Mississippi National River and Recreation Area. This is our seventy-two-mile park, with the Twin Cities sitting like a giant checks and balance for the river to traverse through. (For more information, visit www.nps.gov/miss.)

If you want to experience an enticing day of Twin Cities history, travel to the Mill City Museum and learn how geological and human activity transformed St. Anthony Falls from treacherous waters into native sacred sites, and finally into a manipulated participant of cosmopolitan life. Try to imagine the scale and scope of the prehistoric falls that used to flood all of downtown St. Paul—they rivaled the immensity of other famous falls such as Niagara or Victoria Falls in Zambia. Back around the end of the last Ice Age, St. Anthony Falls had a possible height of two hundred feet and a possible length of up to two miles. Since then, the falls have receded to where they currently reside in Minneapolis.

My quest over the last two years has captivated me and leaves me wanting more knowledge, but more importantly, more of a stake in what happens to the river, especially in Pool 2— the stretch of river from the Ford Dam to the Hastings Dam and the area where my family lives. This area in particular is a critical area for restoration and management following directly after the confluence of the Minnesota and Mississippi Rivers at Fort Snelling and before the waters reach Lake Pepin. It's a "working river"—yes. A river that resembles nothing of the natural sort—yes. A river overrun with agricultural chemicals and silt dredging—to a degree. But those statements aren't the finite condition of the river.

The Mississippi River has come a long way in recent decades. The eagles and other birds of prey have returned after years of detrimental pollutants like DTT and PCBs affected the viability of their eggs. The national ban on these chemicals has helped these populations recover, and is one of the inspirations for my writing.

Walleye, smallmouth bass, and catfish are back in Pool 2—a sign that the river has slowly recovered since the 1972 Clean Water Act. Previous to this monumental legislation a fisherman would be at a loss to find but one fish in the waters downstream of the early 20th Century St. Anthony Falls. (For more information, visit www.mnhs.org/places/safhb.)

Recreation on the river is increasing as well. Environmental efforts are actively ramping up local awareness. Friends of the Mississippi River with their "State of the River" reports, Great River Greening, and Friends of Pool 2 are some of the non-profit groups available to address all river environmental interests.

My writing goal with this poetry collection was rather simplistic in nature. I wanted to write for one year about the river, once every two to three days. It was meant to be a flow-of-consciousness project to soak in the surroundings and also develop my voice. I created about 120 poems that year.

My overarching goal was to use writing as a commitment to observe and learn. It's humbling to be able to watch a juvenile eagle grow to adulthood and try and put those familial sounds and behaviors to paper (hence my "How to Describe the Eagle's Cry" obsession). It's humbling to learn that there are river pelicans. I'm in awe of how their quorum movements— how all the parts move as one—liquefy the sky. Now, when I see them, I wonder how many people know what they are.

I shrink at the overnight flooding events that laugh at our attempts at gates and walls. I watch in awe as fishermen stand on their boats in the wily current and manage to find that walleye mattress. I'm embarrassed at how much I don't know of what passes before my eyes—blackbird rants, food wars, and invasive acorns. Pfeiffer continues on with his ivory-billed woodpecker experience chronicled earlier, advocating for the need of a "chronic passion." I love this quote for its feeling of desperation:

> I don't doubt a persistent human passion for wildlife. Nor do I doubt the distractions keeping us from nature. What we need is a more measured passion, a chronic passion, a broader caring for wildlife beyond charismatic. Sure, we need the pandas and the whales as icons, for posters and fundraising, and for our hearts to beat faster. But so much more wild is out there vanishing or in trouble. We're losing it from under our noses.

This book is part of my take on accepting his challenge.

There's a true world treasure below our bridges. There's a lot of work that needs to be done within the Mississippi River watershed—carp invasion prevention is a notable example. On my own part, there are more fascinating stories about the Mississippi River that must wait for future writing. Perhaps I'll join in the literary conversation on how to perfectly describe that muddy color of brown (many have thrown their oars in on that one).

My answer to those aforementioned questions may not be salient yet, but I can answer in my opinion that the river isn't gross, and yes, we do swim in it. I'm learning what has been done to the river—and many of those stories are success stories too. I haven't eaten a fish from the Mississippi yet, but I would. I see "her" as a reflection of us. We are what we do to our river and water; we are as clean and conscientious as we allow it to be.

Tap in.

1

June

Mississippi Drum

pulse beating in the palm of my hand-
unharnessed skill
the unknown exhilarates and alarms my heart

she plays and she pulls and I reel back in haste,
gripping the cork too tight

she's wiser than me, I'll give her that,
so she takes her time

finally I see her silver-blue body emerge,
fat on the side
pregnant with life and hungry.
she's heavy and full and I can't believe
the work she got out of me.

first fish

6.4.15

Songbird

na na na na na

na na na na na

na na na na na

na na na na na

na na na na na

na na na na na

. . . . na na na na na

Songbird sits near Singer serger—

Singing songs of sewing.

Open window invites

Songbird staccato delights.

6.7.15

Vultures

like an orbiting momentum of connected parts-
a bolas that connects and tethers,
the vultures move as one.
each with missing feathers.

6.20.15

AUTHOR'S NOTE: *"A bolas" is two heavy balls secured on a strong cord, used to throw at animals and entangle their legs.*

New

our giant yellow boat
looks like it could be a float

careening through the Twin Cities Gay Pride Parade

and all the river rats know we're new
she gives us away, one giant yellow clue

their boats are all brown, green, and metal

6.27.15

Dewdrop

torn, the weathered post of yesteryear making

infirmary, cholera, disease basks in the mind's beginning

my childhood, my life, erases slowly behind me, a couple paces aft-

blacken pits slowly fill. I am not a soul tied to the bottom of the river.

Begin by stripping, heavy potassium hydroxide, methylene chloride, old-fashioned scraper,

and then notice the small things next.

stare into a globe, one tiny dewdrop—like a clear sequin shining at 7:00 a.m.

work
your
way
back
up
to
humanity

6.30.15

2

July

July 4th, 2015

July 4th was marked by a hazy river but not unbearable.
I have only found time to remember it now.
Quite surprising, at least in the mid-morning wake-up—how
quiet it seemed on this day.
Barges on vacation begetting kayakers and canoes
that usually don't brave the loud waters.
All I hear is the echoing of a peaceful conversation gently
traveling the wrong way up the river.

A week or so before, we discovered a hidden aeronautical landing
strip
down a backwater slough. (The river is an obvious home to sea-
faring planes,
but I never knew it.)
Home of a bright amphibious Cessna hidden in the trees, sleeping
under a shed.
These small aircrafts cycle on and off the river, practicing
landing and taking off
at low traffic times. But not today. Today she sleeps.

Gladly we discover catfish back there too.
My little one names the first fish Earl—worried he would get
lonely she next asks to put the small crappie with him.

The eagles seem lazy,
sitting uncharacteristically side-by-side on one branch in the
cottonwood that
towers over all else.
Surveying one direction of the river, each.

Others comment on the insufferable commotion of fireworks
in town,
but there is none of that here.

My brother is "live" in a *New York Times* video discussing banning
the southern confederate flag,
and I sit here wondering how much weight and meaning we put
into symbols, and why.

7.4.15

Giant

We moved to the river last fall.
Winter covered her over, but good.
Now eagles pass me with a laissez-faire passing glance,
I am grounded to the earth.

We moved to the river last fall.
Wish I knew how to tap into the lives that grow when we're not
looking.
It's a mystery to me.
I am a giant disrupting the Earth.

7.9.15

Blackbird Racket

Overwhelming racket.

Whether in
the electric air,

your mind,

or the blackbirds
that litter the sound waves with calls of alarm.

Our society castigates one,

ignores the other,

and venerates the third based on its inclusion to nature.

The chaos we choose to let in

any given moment,

turns to summations over time and defines who we are,

at any given moment.

7.9.15

How To Describe the Eagle's Cry: Take 1

brushed upstroke staccatos
calling to their lovers and birthed

then descending vibrato staircases
sentries of the earth

one breath hugs the next
drops that come and go

back 'n forth across the river
airborne eagle's tic-tac-toe

7.10.15

Dead Raccoon

He marched slowly from the wood

where the expanse of the current swept aft and south.

No more battles left to beat,

the last man standing in defeat.

Head held high,

he went as far as he could muster.

Sound of lapping came in clusters.

The smell of spring reminding him of home.

The spell of moonlight to carve his tomb.

He made it as far as the Dallas star

then, right there in our backyard,

lay down to take his final rest,

his hand held bravely at his chest.

7.14.15

AUTHOR'S NOTE: This poem is written as an homage to the summer of raccoon deaths
in our neighborhood. I know most think they are a nuisance, but when you find them
sleeping their eternal death next to your recently planted garden bed, called the Dallas
Star, stretched along their backs, faces masked, and their tiny little hands too preciously
cute, it made me wonder how long they suffer before making it all the way across our lawn.

River Lock 3

What would the river say if it could speak?

Would it gracefully bow out of duty,

buckle under the pressure and weep?

Would it speak to the sigmoidal flying pelicans

upon their landing in the shallows?

That locks and dams bracing the shores

are forms of river gallows?

7.19.15

The Wind Is a Force that Cannot Be Stopped

the wind is a force that cannot be stopped

granting the water permission to do its bidding

what once was a gentle promenade is now

wily and alive and thrashing us about in its swells

it seeps into everything no matter the precautions we take

it makes a mockery of the shutters and whistles in warnings

it has no intention of letting up

it throws our towels overboard and away and threatens to take more

it keeps me from eating, it keeps me from thinking

it keeps me staring at him across the way, frozen in a trance
created by my muffled ears

I have seen this invisible force send sheet metal through tree trunks

and litter Styrofoam stuffing onto bare twigs after a tornado

the wind is a force that cannot be stopped

it sets fire to anything it chooses

7.23.15

Night Sky

we danced with abandon

like nothing had ever hurt us before

we were the ones they look at from afar, wishing

we raised our hands to the sky

and made a time we will never forget

the heavens smiled down on us

relief and release and joy finally returning

after a long dark winter

7.24.15

How to Describe the Eagle's Cry: Take 2

not a songbird
nor a coo

not a caw
nor a whistle

not silent like an owl
nor knocking

not signaling the dawn
nor signaling the day

a broken wheel
a rusty revolution

a hand-cranked machine that has seen better days
air out of a tire

a relief from duty
poignant and purposeful

and it fades away

7.24.15

Two Fawns

teleported in broad daylight

from nowhere they emerge

slivers of mirage

they can sense me through glass and mortar

turning sliver-side toward me so I have to look twice

now we both hold our breaths

I know I can win.

the slightest twitch in one ear and they're onto me

a silent communiqué humans will never know—
alerts the other to my presence

they jump up and to the side, brazen and impatient-
still

exposing their vulnerable brown bellies and tail—
like the reckless kids they are

they pepper back and forth across the yard and into the wood

7.30.15

Not Our River

Lost my shoes.
Lost my son.

No more drinking water for anyone.

Bruised right wrist.
Scraped left arm.

Right-but-quick this river has lost all charm.

7.31.15

AUTHOR'S NOTE: This poem was written during a family trip where we went tubing down the Cannon River at the Welch Mill after torrential rains created a high river. This describes the aftermath of a head-on collision with a flotilla of lackadaisical afternoon drinkers all tied together like a giant honeycombed tribe. I thought my children and I were going to die as they ran us over on some tiny rapids. Luckily I lived to tell the tale.

3

August

How to Describe the Eagle's Cry: Take 3

the young eagle skirmished about the lower trees below the
mighty cottonwood for weeks.

bleating and bleeding incessantly
my anthropomorphic view granted him feelings for his mother—
a wanting to be let back under her wing
looking up at his mother
whose steely gaze never left the river
he cried for mercy
first in the cedar
then from the burr oak
next from the windmill
then standing awkwardly on the green Adirondack chair

I reasoned he must be in lesson
surely his mother has some grace—
"stay near me dear, choose your own tree, below mine."

but today a different story emerged altogether
this boy grew to beast
his black shadow dwarfing everything
today he bleated nonstop!
like the blackbird racket from before
finally he mustered his play

he had been dreaming it for weeks.

like never before
he swept up to the mighty cottonwood
just shy of where Father held his throne —proudly looked over
their Universe

landing low, son sirened straight up
demanding to be heard
never closing wing

Dad's sharp beak and girth came into view as he looked over his
shoulder.
nervousness is all I could name
son lunged for the alpha
knocking him from the tree
primping into position and taking post over prey

silent for a while—
a day's work done by eight—
he lazily releases four or five low guttural calls
curdled and indiscriminate
the trees were then quiet
no fussing
and order was made

8.2.15

River Lock 2

people are nicer to you
up here on River Lock 2

they wave with zest as we pass on by,
all they want to share is a nice and pleasant "hi"

so different from River Lock 3-
where all the boaters just let you be,

where yachts grow up and sprout,
blue water of the Croix no doubt

transient lease on their clear blue,
the whole time deep inside we all knew-

that while it was nice to visit River Lock 3,
we return to our 2 with pride and glee

hightail it on back to our mud,
clipping those logs with a thud

where warmth comes from within and then out
we've carved out a spot on the river, no doubt

8.3.15

Here Comes a Barge: Take 1

I feel it first—
before she's even near me

Deep in the earth—
connecting to my heartbeat

If she's small—
it's faint, grows stronger if she's large

This is how you know:

Here
Comes
A
Barge!

We yell,
"Barge!"

In Missouri it's much longer:
"Git outta the way!"
When the current's a'growin' stronger

Maria
Georgette
Nina
True Blue

Named after their lovelies so far removed.

8.6.15

Pileated Woodpecker

pill
eee
ate
ted
wood
peck
ers
rap
rap
rapping
at a tree
no one's home inside the hollows
but he
raps
incessantly
bash
bash
bashing
beak and head
the commotion it must cause
our brains would be rattlin'
begging for a pause

pill
eee
ate
ted
wood
peck
ers
elusive in the breeze
do not take
one step closer
lest they fidget, fret, and flee

fan of brilliant feathers
tropical birds of the North
flying oil paintings
swaths of color coming forth

8.10.15

Time Warping Is a Rush

I now love the beach
more than I ever have before
saved from our fate
pristine and basic, left unrestored
left back in time
before addiction took us hard
saved from the future
where all pastimes, now marred

a respite from our techie obsessions
kids playing in the dirt
mom is shaking "two minutes left, kids"
young lovers there to flirt
kinda sad this is novel
what the heck did we do?
in our hearts we all grovel
for the simpler life we once knew

toddlers hiding under towel forts
nets for sand
or fish
or
whatever
splash, or chase, or float
we could stay here all day,
or maybe forever

one sole radio proves the year
just enough to keep it cool
we share in this revelry
the music is just a tool
did we fall into 1950
did this not happen to us?
happy to be simple—
time warping is a rush

8.12.15

How to Become a Poet

Dickenson's coveted silence—
thoughts

la petite mort or the little death
a fleeting loss of contact with reality—
perspective

Dante's dark wood
where the straightaway was lost—
sorrow

that is how you become a poet

8.13.15

Breathe in Deep

Oh, that smell you grow to love
When the August sun first hits the mud
Faint fish-gut odor in the air
Sand and seaweed mixed in layers
A sign that summer's been long baking
Water levels dropped, no escaping

Drive on down
This gets steep

What you've found
Breathe in deep

8.16.15

Death of a Friend

lo, she strikes again
impregnating the mind
inhaling all the whispers
so no one can hear

and what remains:
her black storm that comes in waves

riptorn damage at the bow
the point most forward
is surely lost
when ship sets way,

losing compass, light, and will
her black storm now reduced to swill

8.24.15

Rain in the River

Every drop fills the tub
Fills her up
Up she comes
She grows stronger
Grows with each drop
Dropping water
Water's drop

8.18.15

Spider's Haiku

spiders swing in skies:

sewing slingshots, lines, and slides.

summer. sunset. smiles.

8.22.15

Ode to Mississippi: Take 1

The Nile
The Amazon
The Yangtze
It saddens me what they did to the Yangtze . . .
> *Three Gorges Dam, baiji river dolphin*
> *—did you know there was once a river dolphin?*

And the MISSISSIPPI!

This working river, this masterpiece

If you zoomed out, away from Earth,
this fourth largest river could be seen from space.
I don't even know if that's true—
but I imagine it is

The only habitable planet in our galaxy and this is the fourth of
all the waterways
—a waterway for aliens to dream about
—a waterway to connect cultures that are hours and days and
  decades apart
—a waterway that made Twain famous,
> *Pudd'nhead Wilson, Huckleberry, Sawyer*
> *—have you read what "marking twain" means?*

Then why does she get not a passing glance from most?
a stinky, up-turned nose at the mention of her name
surely she deserves
more revelry and fame

8.27.15

AUTHOR'S NOTE: The Three Gorges Dam is located in the city of Yichang, China on the Yangtze River. The Yangtze is the third longest river in the world and the construction of the dam has been controversial for the ecological impacts it bestows on the natural ecology of the river.

4

September

Missing Motorbike

me, night, motorbike
High Smith bridge covered in lights
high hell smells and sights

9.3.13

Attack of the Red Oak

What was once a friend,

now foe,

as we try to cross the field.

Watch overhead,

watch close

as she waits for your approach.

Spitfire launching

on toe-breaking

sidewalk paths.

We long for a trip

to the garage,

that's happy and relaxed.

Run for cover

but beware,

the red squirrel is on her side,

a sentinel on duty—

he owns his job with *ferocious* pride.

Acorn bullets,

haphazard debris

am I crazy,

or is this tree laughing at me?

9.7.15

Hummingbird

I was walking along my path one day
when a hummingbird stopped me in my tracks.
It said, "Where are you going in such a rush?"
I said, "Excuse me, I have to pass."

I held my attention to the sky,
looking for the great and mighty raptors.
The hummingbird tried once more:
"Wow, your attention sure is captured."

The little levitator gave up in short
and went along its way.
I hurried up my path unhindered
to see what eagles may.

A little too loud and a little too late,
my haste had pushed the eagles out.
I looked back to at least be amused with the hummingbird,
but it was found nowhere about.

9.8.15

The Sog

the sog penetrates the air
turns our bread to mold
in fewer days
a mini San Fran—
Mississippi sourdough
soft sedum
moss happily grows out of August
blue mist canopies-
driving out of the valley
the sun roils the low-flung mist
slowly burning it off-
all morning long
the weighted landing of animals into grass and trees
ka-thunk-
thicker than any other time of summer
echos of sound
acute and closer

saturation

9.10.15

Waterway

the way in which water connects us all,

a landmass migration storms the earth,

we are knit together

by streams, to rivers, to seas, to oceans,

a drop in time travels along a waterway,

reaching our hearts, born as one

9.16.15

Decibel Levels

Sit still outside for a while
and notice the dial turning

slowly

up . . .

A world buttons up when the human arrives.

Tune in to Decibel Level 1:
A brave lone bird.

Level 2:
Bird's conversation.

Level 3:
The highway from here?
I never knew it.

Level 4:
What the wind says to the trees.

Level 5:
The slow churn of a train revving up to depart.

6:
Dried leaves stirring.

7:
Hair, brushing over ears.

8:
The once free and roaming bulldog now home, seldom barking, dog's domain.

9:
Woodpecker.

10:
Door slamming shut.
                    Blackbird attack.
                                  Lone honeybee.
                                      Frantic
squirrels, wind-chimes, and even the pileated woodpecker testing the water.
                How
                   do all living creatures know
                that
          We
        Are
      Predators
    and
   are
  to
 be
feared?

9.17.15

Coyotes

I slept outside to be closer to nature.
Fool!
How close do you want to be?
Awoken
in an instant,
by a lost child in the woods,
seemingly close,
edge of the wood.
Perhaps a bit beyond,
then one begets two—
two crying lost children
in a haze.
Am I dreaming?
No.
What are children doing in the woods?
It must be so late.
What has happened in the world?
They sound so sad,
so lost.
A train cries-
the children follow,
crying out in pain.
Louder.
Constant.
So sad.

Two begets four or five.
They blend their cries for the train with small
nearly inaudible howls—
A gathering.
I lie wide awake in the dark,
afraid to pull back the curtain.
Louder and louder as the train passes by:
cacophony, howling and crying.
Meeting down below the limestone bluff.
the train ends then,
silence.
Empty island in the marsh,
children back to sleep.
While I myself,
will sleep
wide-awake this night.

9.20.15

Blood Moon

coyotes beckon the blood moon
howling with the ascent
eclipse,
being taken over by darkness
universal pull—
instinct
or
simply
a coincidence

9.28.15

5

October

October

Wake up in October to cold floorboards on our feet,
scrambling to find slippers, socks, but sandals still abound!
And the wind howling its way through the door,
scurry into the kitchen to warm my hands on the coffee cup.
Sweater already, frantic to find four for all the littles,
walk past the bed, placing hands under the covers, still holding
heat from the night before,
wishing to get back into floating warm feathers and dreamscape,
but duty calls.
Breath catches in the air and pauses before dissipating,
"It's cold out here!" our son yells back as he rushes to the bus.
Run the hot faucet to thaw the hands for typing—
summer has finally timed out.

10.2.15

How to Describe the Trains: Take 1

trains rock on by
racing time against the clock

blaring unceremoniously to the wild wind
it does not, it will not,
ever stop

blare, blare! at the wide blue moon
unsettling deer from covens, coyotes, babies too
reminding us there's a deadline
growing up from baby's *choo-choo!*

get too close and feel it in your bones
the reverberance travels far
clicks for miles that communicate power
ghostly locks and metal bars

something about it warns us to stay our ground
don't get too close, yet also
not too far
A mystery lies within each one
dormant, hidden—
miles of colorful cars

10.6.15

The Fence

There exists a fence
Off over yonder
Old weathered wood posts
A place we often ponder

Slag wire connects the wood
Wind whips right on through
Been dividing us forever now
We go there to learn the truth

We've met at this line before
You stand just on the other side
We face each other at the fence
The laws of property we abide

A place to know our dualism
A place we go to stew
A place we know is trusted
To keep dividing me from you

I stand in the dusty dirt looking over
I stand there remembering the truth—
We once grew up together
What do we have to lose?

How hard would it be to meet at the line?
How hard to clip the wire?
Is it possible to meet in the middle?
Is this what people desire?

10.7.15

River

On the highway-waterway
here at my fingertips—
let 'er rip.
Here is the source of life
so go on, take a sip.
Real.
Not transient, not a trick.
Often the life you get
is the one you pick.
Don't waste time or be too slow.
The river waits for no one—
we, of anyone,
should know.

Beckoning,
calling,
the river gradual
and free.

Be still
Be comfortable
Be you
Just
Be.

Or toss all woes into its greedy mouth.
Let them all go.
Point them to their destination—
far away,
the Deep South.

The power of the current,
ceaseless and strong.
You have no strength to fight it,
been holdin' on too long.
Courage to open your hands,
your heart,
with all washed away,
let the river fill you with a fresh new start
no sedimental record to lead you astray.

You once promised yourself
to not place love on a shelf,
you would let it run wild,
run far,
run free . . .

Be still
Be comfortable
Be anything
Be you
Be
Free.

Go in for a soak,
giving way to the vortex.
Eddies, the undertow—
let your ambitions float

Then all will be dissolved
lying in the sun-gleaming glitter.
This is your life, after all,
and not just a river.

10.20.14

The 45-Degree October Tilt

sun slanting in at a sharp angle
throwing rays in my face
flickering tree limbs at my retinas
flashing strobe lights and shadows
I scowl in the reflection
angry with its assault
don't do this
don't go yet
we have only had a short while with you
I need to get back to the beach
I need to sleep on our hill
I need to find that giant yellow carp again

10.12.15

Dorothy

Wind like today
Swept poor Dorothy away
Gone with the summer, needles, and shutters.

Can I toss my woes in there too?
Ready to think something new.
What a good use of the weather.

10.12.15

Mauve

Mauve isn't a color
It's a condition
Looking at the bathroom tile and
She keeps wishin'
Keep the cold at bay
Keep the sun shining in
Wishin' the snow isn't where we are
But where we've been
Maybe if she paints it all yellow
Keep singing to the sun with salutes
Husband hugs her in real close:
"Winter's coming—and it's all moot"

10.18.15

Boat for a Home

claiming stake
claiming home
regretting you packed up
everything you own
hedged all bets
this is the one
no more worries
life in the sun

feelin' sorry for you now
as the wind takes you over
no more wishing to be done
on a four-leaf clover
dear little spider
I'm sorry I must bemoan
but why'd you go off
and pick a boat for your home?

10.25.15

AUTHOR'S NOTE: A tiny spider spent all night, October 24th to be exact, creating a masterpiece of real estate, but unfortunately the chosen location was on a sidebar, on a boat, exposed to the elements and unsheltered from the ensuing wind that blew his house to the river. I hope he made it out of the ordeal and built a new home on a rafter somewhere.

6

November

Raking Leaves: Take 1

Find and use the benefits
of local

gravity—

a quick dip,
the ease of the fall,

we need everything it offers, its entire momentum

and sprawl.

11.3.15

AUTHOR'S NOTE: *Every year during leaf season I am very grateful for a circuitous and short retaining wall that aids in moving leaves from up high to down low, and hence closer to our trailer for a windy trip to the compost site. Yes, even to the point of writing a poem about it.*

Raking Leaves: Take 2

tsunami of leaves
I'm drowning
left deltoid splitting into three
throbbing
the middle one jumping forward, on the verge of leaving
leafing—our new business
and then
begging
to be released from impending duty
yet
mercy nowhere to be found
because as formidable as the sky is long, they extend far across
the ground
crispy forevers
one million promises I keep
to be your guardian,
great oaks

. . . raking leaves sucks!
maples are better, fluffy
but you, you cling to the earth like you don't want to leave
and perspire, you cry, making a sloshy matted mud pile that
moves as one loathsome brick

I lay back to drink in the dusty air,
> "rake them to the river," the laborer emphatically states,
> passing me by
> "why waste your time with loading, and driving and
> paying?"
> he throws his pile to the river, claps his hands in a
> singsong *see? so easy.*

rake it to the river, I'll rake you . . .

we're trying to do this differently, so it's worth it . . .
ahh forget it
never mind
we love it
we really do

11.15.15

Raking Leaves: Take 3

Service to the
oaks
One billion backbend
strokes
Graced by reprieve from
snow
To rake then lift and
throw

But don't grin prematurely
More in the spring assuredly

Duty to towering still warriors out back
Kilojoules are burning, now that's a fact

11.18.15

Fervor—stillness

flocking to the water
enticed by a river they must share
racing to deliver
voracious with their wares
over the horizon they churn
ramping up the charge

sure to beat the ice
that threatens the
ignited barge
long will be the winter
long will be the chill
nexus for the spring
eager upon a captain's will
silenced, ole Mississippi
soon to emerge again

11.30.15

AUTHOR'S NOTE: This is an acrostic poem where the first letter of each line spells a word, in this case, the title. 'Fervor' describes how the captains of the barges ramp up their cargo trips at the end of the season—the river is constantly shaking with waves due to the traffic. The industry is racing against the silence that will come from the first freeze. The first freeze inhales all activity and holds its breath for winter.

7

December

The Buck that Came to Town

Turning left, then veering right,
we head on home
to seal in the night.
Hot pot on,
dinner is warm,
gray mist and drips,
all trees forlorn.

Then he appears in the
distance.
You look at me
and
I look at you.
Rolling to a stop
you ask,
Now what do we do?

Brazen guy, he seems,
standing so proud.
Chest puffed out
and waxen antlers loud.
Nonchalant,
he supplants the norm,
moved into town,
avoiding the storm.

Gun shots fire
steady
not far from his ears
Yet, he's been doing this, now,
for quite a
few years.

A regular old civilian
no hunters can come 'round.
A regular old Buck,
our resident of the town.

12.8.15

Who Wants to Read About the Winter?

It's hard to write in the winter.
What's an author meant to do?
Try and find a little inspiration,
but green life, olfactory delights,
bated breath in steamy nights,
lightening bugs,
crickets too,
sun-kissed shades,
who needs shoes!
Hands in dirt,
birth above and below,
emerging creatures—
grown from snow.

. . . .

but they all sleep.
I have a
chip on my shoulder,
and winter's cheap.

Bah!
I could write about the stillness.
I could comment on the gray.
I could comment straight to April,
but there is nothing good to say.

Now hear this!
I am selling barren wastelands.
I am selling the color brown.
I am selling stock in what I have—
endless blocks of frozen ground.

12.12.15

Squirrel (Rat)

squirrel (rat) takes refuge
under an arborvitae
shakes the rain collected from his tail
his efforts were not in vain

acorn trails

moss and grass exposed to air
he finds more of what he needs
little rat with squirrel-like face
you travel the raining sheets of silver

you're so commonplace

12.14.15

One Wet December

"Well that there is one wet December.

Do you ever recall such a sight!?

This is *voodoo weather.*

Well heck! Yesterday, I coulda ridden my bike!

Didja hear on the news how much we've gotten?

How much snow do you think this would be!?

(Interrobangs on weather changes)

Sure beats the heck out of me!"

12.14.15

AUTHOR'S NOTE: *The interrobang is a clever mix of half "What?" and half "What!"
I think it describes ninety-nine percent of my reactions to all things presented to me
on Earth. Maybe in other galactispheres I would resort to the guillemets or the full
stops more often.*

Chisel and Widen the Chasm

I could start today,
living on a bluff,
continue the work.
Find my good gloves.

Lacerate the wall
that follows the riverway.
Keep my chisel working nonstop,
all through the night and
into day.

Break my land off
from the rest.
It's my land, after all,
I earned it best.

Fracture the lines
that connect me
to town.
Forget your names.
This is my ground.

If I could cut the earth
right on through,
then you'd certainly know
this land is for me,
not for you.

If I could live
on a limestone island,
all my own,
I could revel in
the isolation skills
that over a lifetime I have honed.

It's a rather large chunk—
I'd better start today.
I don't want someone coming over
thinking I ought to do it their way.

Working on my island,
the next step is to make it fly.
Or send it down the river—
I don't really care
if I have to make this bluff cry.

Yes,
alone is best.
I can trust everyone there.
Alone at rest.
What do I care?

12.15.15

8

January

That Was Only Yesterday

coated in a stark powdery blue
a spell takes over
anything that moves
electrified by the struggling sun
defying gravity
the flakes descend
one by one
taking their time
a talent for
arresting human attention

one

two

three

the time of year that time forgot
and the snowflakes
that slowly drop
yesterday the steam rose from across the river
like a hasty fire made on the island
water scrambling for breath
overtaken with a deep sleep
where are the eagles now?
how can they rest?
whitetails escaped across the grays
and that was
only
yesterday

1.11.2016

Mother Watching Child Get on the Bus

you find yourself waiting for
the moment
leaning on the doorframe,
arms crossed.
Time is bait.

warm condensate
on the frozen glass
breath audible,
now you became
the one who waits.

invested in
the moment,
owning your current fate,
wishing to pry yourself free,
but now its too late.

a test of time.
Time is the rate.
holding a post now,
quivering thoughts,
quivering thoughts,
they quack.

imagining the finish,
oh! waiter of the ones who wait,
not enough,
you have to see it!
you're arrested in
waiting's fate.

you find yourself waiting for
the moment
leaning on the doorframe,
arms crossed.
Time is bait.

no one else is here to do it,
you have become
the one who waits.

1.14.16

Neruda Was Right

it's a *hush,*
hush,
here
in my corner of the world,
German-descendant farmers
quietly tuck in for the long winter.
the minuscule drops
blanket our 'scape
be still, be silent,
they whisper
as we are tucked away
like the shire,
unknowing of what lies beyond our hills,
our rolling river.
we eat our canned jams
and wait.
the snow says *hush,*
hush,
and today I think
Neruda was right.
I scoffed at his poem, my first
go with his words, and I
refused to believe
his judgment that
electronics
enslave humans was
true.

I refused his pointed finger
and thought,
who are you?
last night,

MPR covered the Congo.
20,000
and more
slaves living in holes.
mining my gold.
women taken from
within and men from
without.
so I can write this,
so I can text you,
so we can magnetize our thoughts
toward the glowing light of
now.
Neruda was right.
and my snow falls so slow,
whispering *hush,*
hush.

1.21.16

9

February

Transient Stillness Captured on the Mississippi Mornings

on a steep inhale,
held breath,
upside-down
reflection,
a perfectly poised still frame
the river says
look up

exhale
for the
right-side up
and the tremors
of water
begin again

2.1.16

Something to Be Sold

Hackles are up.
My ears bend toward the
recessed wind.

Reading between lines
I search, I listen,
dissecting intent.

A long-winded revolution
in the way—

I
have
been
here
before.

Someone tries to sell you something,
you buy again and again.
Then what have we learned
if it's all the same?

But, it is not,
and I am not.

Because time gently
nudges us off the cliff
of each second
and we can never go back.

Reality is in our
perceptions.

That, is it.

This time, take a new action,
You've learned a lot.

Rest those weary wolf eyes.
Straighten your gaze on the
far and faint
horizon
and go.

2.8.16

Hawaiian Sunrise

Lucky,
a Hawaiian sunrise,
and if I close my eyes
I can sort of surmise,
that warm sunny day.

A mere three degrees,
shaking at the knees,
but with a small warm breeze
to whisk me across the sea.

Look up, don't look down,
sherbet orange and golden crowns
in the sky, there are no frowns,
make sure to stay above the horizon.

For if you mistake,
that snow for a lake,
hypothermia you cannot fake.
Frozen is an unpleasant lesson.

2.10.16

Pileated Woodpecker: Take 2

so you fly again in February,
scalloping through the brisk wind,
the noncommittal type,
flaky,
and
a flight risk.
following the two white circles,
a reverse domino—
a black kite—
from worn, wooden light post
to the next.
when I approach
you hide your head.
a tiny boxer,
weaving from left to right.
I still see you,
and again you are off
in flight.

2.11.16

Ode for Black Holes

Two black holes collide into one.
On the event horizon they meet.
First, twenty-nine times the size of the sun,
Seven more, the second, mere beats.

From chaos and disorder, destruction unwinds,
The rise of life and peace.
Albert guessed it before other minds
(His math turned out to be dece').

Surges of gravity created some ripples,
The needles, in an odd way, now bent.
Like sheets on the line, time's fabric of dimples
Laps, creases, and crimps.

More akin to the beloved Land of Never,
Ageless we are, proof that Barrie was clever.

C. Williams & B. Williams
2.15.16

Giant Spoons

Giant spoons
Giant spoons everywhere.

Where do all the little ones go?
From their sprouts, the big ones grow.

Fork and knife and straws in June,
What I really want is a decent-sized spoon.

2.17.16

Two Eagles Cross

Two eagles cross
over a bridge one day.
One headed north,
the second headed
the other way.

One was off to find
warmer water,
one to find
more fish.
One was bound
to find true love,
one to glide, swoop,
and swish.
Thinking a thought
as though one might,
one bird began to
start off in flight.

Thinking for a while
as though one may,
the other began to
travel and stray.

But if I could
reach up
and grab hold of either ear,

I would whisper,

It's the same river,
I'll save you the
travel and
distance,
my dear.

2.19.16

Light

Remember,
a single candle—
nearing expiration
and placed inside
an autumn jack-o'-lantern—
flickers, desperate for air.
The ever-present wind of
a worn-out revolving
carousel relic
St. Paulians salvaged and hid
amongst the high-rises and skyways.
It reflects a white light off old mirrors, a
dancing display across the black walls behind us.
A light probe held to a motorcycle
to check timing,
a wanting connection,
a corroded battery line.
We huddle in a cold, dimly lit garage,
breathing on our fingers,
vying for a two-by-four to stand on
that's warmer than the concrete floor.
Now, at dusk, dark snow rolls in,
quickens across the barren spaces of our yard,
speeding past a few small lights—
no time to spare.
Sideways, the frozen drops race on to
another place.

Glittering prisms
flashing with a desperate pulse to
warn us of what is ahead.
Take cover, the flakes
look back and whisper
as they cruise on by.
Dancing shapes,
wandering light,
twinkles glimmer,
making winter bright.

2.22.16

AUTHOR'S NOTE: *This poem mentions the lights of the Cafesjian's Carousel, a famed heroic story of St. Paul history. Our Fair Carousel Inc. is a non-profit you can check out to keep this local treasure shiny like a new penny. See it now at Como Zoo. I used to see it in Town Square Park as a child.*

10
March

Dust on Our Hearts

dust on our hearts,

what of it anymore,

flick of the wrist,
check the clock,
catch the train,

while our hearts,

they stop

3.15.16

Return of the Tugboat

the way you enter
my room
is shocking.
unannounced
and
so sudden:
there you are.
and I startle more than once this
week at your unapologetic presence.
from the darkness
a single beacon shining,
you announce
Here I am!
and
See me now!
jerking me away from
the safe haven of dreams
to capture my full attention
like a child, a puppy,
an emergency.
bold of you—
while I
scramble to make sense
of the light,
quiet my fight or flight,
ease the surge of adrenaline
that makes me scared of you

at the start,
then next,
caught naked,
from the shower
in the dark,
your soft light
plays tricks with my eyes
and there you are

casting moving shadows
all across my room,
like a ghost
playing hide-and-seek,
a few seconds more
you shine heavenly
white light
straight through these walls
searching for my eyes in each
window
as you pass by safely
through the water
upstream
chartering your way
to the port in St. Paul

3.16.16

11

April

Walk Through The Rose Garden

Why do you walk
through the rose garden?

Is the path alongside
not as nice?

I cringe at your
path chosen.

Wouldn't this path
over here suffice?

Why do you walk
through the rose garden?

Are your eyes
not as keen as mine?

You always go off the path,
and it gets me every time.

4.2.16

AUTHOR'S NOTE: *The initial inspiration here was our puppy, Tugboat, a French Bulldog that seemed to prefer to walk straight through the thorny bushes instead of the grass or sidewalk. Further meaning, for me, are the people in my life that push the envelope constantly and precariously hang their livelihoods in the balance.*

Morning on the Mississippi: Take 1

a fabric
from my window
I see Red, Black,
Blue, and Gray

the sun begins on the
western Mississippi riverbank
a deep Red band
a solid swath
delineating night from day

the trees start out on fire
down below
the fish still sleep
in a steely Blue darkness
the low banks too
time to stir
and rise
to meet the rays

4.9.16

Morning on the Mississippi: Take 2

she's a fierce one today
giving them nothing
on their quest
pushing
pushing
to move cold
and stagnant spring goods
steel plates and
power toward
the rear
waves lashing where boat meets—
with a smile
she steely greets:

"Go ahead and try it,
save none of your
gas and time this day.
I push in the way I want.
It's best for you
to bend my way.

My army of whitecaps
tirelessly march on,
They never tire,
like the steel you keep,
summoning you to stand still
with my cool and magical sweep."

4.14.16

Why the River

no stop signs,
no street lights
no billboards
stating
McDonald's
at the
next right.

if I have an interest,
if the river
serves my pleasure,
no phone call
aft a few
moments,
requesting a
survey
of my leisure.

no timeline
no deadline
no white line
nor dashed,
the only line I see
is the line
that I cast.

she speaks in
only wind
and of course,
also water
she's usually
quiet—
unless flooding
then I bow,
humbled,

as one of her
daughters

4.16.16

Pelicans Sing a Classical Song

The pelicans sing a
classical song,
widening
curves
on streams
of air.
First
in groups
of three or
four,
stream a
tunnel,
past where
eagles dare.
Tiny specks,
they go up so high.
I love this song, by and by.

4.19.16

Offering of Worms

A good wife
knows the
trade.
In hearts
of love,
where love is
made,
in the offering
of worms.
Plucking tails
from dirt,
his smile
broad,
he stops
and wipes hands
on shirt—
an invite
to take a
break.
An eye
wink
no winking
makes,
start toward
the water,
and crave
to disconnect.
The worms
are flowers
for around
your neck.

4.21.16

Herbert Stuck in a Tree

Dear little brown thing,
what do I call you?
muskrat
beaver
groundhog
hedgehog

From the depths of the earth
you wait for a deep
overcast cloud,
you love rain,
you raise suspicious eyes,
and escape to the tunnels and
drains.
Sorry for the puppy—
he's working on
his bark.
Now you're stuck
on the side of a tree,
you look as if I hung up my old phone,
in the middle of a city park.

Dear Herbert,
little brown thing,
you are so cute,
the way your bump goes
through the grass.
Seeing you makes me smile as the days meander past.

I think I love you,
I cannot lie,
'cept for that one day
when you tried to come inside.
As much as I would hold you tight—
it's my warmth, my library, my right.

4.28.16

1 2

May

Wake up to the Eagle's Call

wake up to the
eagle's call, a
lord presiding
over all.

in the
cottonwood
perched over
everyone
and
everything.
I am
king,
it sings and
sings.

breast held
high
looking left,
looking
right
sharp eyes
to the sky
taking
time in
flight.

smaller
birds skip
up to its
perch
a dark cloud
of noise
assessing their
worth.

tying
ribbons over
water

to and fro
a baker
kneading
air like
dough.

wake up to the
eagle's call, a
lord presiding
over all.

5.2.16

City River

up the river
not very far
they sort metal;
a hungry mouth
places large steel
broken beams
metal softballs
metal sand
into neat piles
day in day out
the smoke is yellow
and gray

up the river
closer now
they clean oil
grids of pipes
stretch the long way
and then up
metal yurts
vats of source
their smoke is an
endless fire
reaching to the birds

a port sits past and down
the only sign on the river
says *pipeline here*
no idling
this port pushes and pulls
filling and draining
train cars, water cars,
trucks
this smoke is the start of the
machines in the morning
dry belts
engine plumes

she's inherited the gruesome
backbone of modern life
most will only see while
passing over a bridge
disgusted by the sight
of the bland pallet that
industrialization
brings to your senses
or turned away by the
putrid stagnant
odors our never-
sleeping American
dreams demand

we've had our grips on
her long and hard
but "nature is red
in tooth and claw"
with an instinct
for balance

5.6.16

Finding The Mattress: Take 1

The mattress
is not a place
where you sleep.

This mattress
is where walleye
typically
keep.

Deep down under
in the recess
of black
calm,

The mattress,
compared to the
river,
is the size
of your
palm.

Finding this mattress
is not a stumble
in the dark.

And it rocks hard
over walls,
wing dams,
wood bark.

No warm
kiss goodnight,
no soft pillow
to catch your head.

Against all odds
wind
current
widow-makers,
this mattress
is no bed.

5.8.16

The River Swells

a
swelling is
an event
that takes
our
breath away,
a primordial
appreciation
that
we have
witnessed
the
calling
each time
in awe
like
fire
for the
first time—
whoa,
she's alive
it's alive
we are
alive.

5.10.16

While Ontario Burns

Opaque gauze over everything I see, faintly the trees, how beautiful something
destructive can be, my eyes start to burn, but this new
filter—I can't stop
It's like a dream, everything softer, pearls
rolling, whispers
I rub my eyes from sleep, step through a frame missing its screen,
how a tilt in perspective can change everything—what is the
most beautiful something can be
and Ontario
the forest is ablaze, we get on with the morning in Minnesota
gazing at the haze.

5.25.16

A Girl without A Boat

Standing parallel to a long and windy pier
no boat in sight
only something in my bones,
something's not right.
For it's a longing not easily described.
A girl without a boat
A girl without pride?
How to sail on—
I have no sail,
Wind, yes—bits—but
no gasoline, no shaded bends, no cold lips.
How to amass notes about my local heron?
I have no notes.
My summer's looking barren.
I know so little
and time is sweet.
What can I sell
to start my fleet?
To meet her in the morning
and meet her in the sun.
To learn all her secrets.
To see where she runs.

5.24.16

13

June

Do Not Be Confused— This Is a Robin's World

Do not be confused.

This is a robin's world.

Fierce mother,
protector and defender.
She waits for me
in the early spring days
scanning trees, waiting, watching.
She meets me in the
garage, swooping in,
levitating,
warning me
not to
pull that crap
again.
Her yard.
Her gazebo.
Her door.
I'm warning you.
Yip yip rat-tat grrrazz ha!
What if you push it?
She will dive-bomb like a
kamikaze crusader.
What does she care?
She told you!

You have been warned!
She has her rights.
Your head is hers.
Don't walk toward that nest.
Don't threaten the tiny blues.
Deep swaths of
might.

Just try to eat a meal
out there, try
to ignore her plight.

Don't be confused.

This is a robin's world.

6.2.16

Each Season

Each season
a chapter unto itself.
Second summer ago,
the great floods.
Iron gates
laid like paper plates thrown
to the wayside.
The river rose,
rock walls crumbled,
and our grass turned to
a sandy beach.
After mid-summer
she finally receded.

Last summer,
summer of love,
we weeded and wed,
eagles married
over their birthed.
Tugboats and barges
were hasty and loud.
Fluttering wings, mites, and
minds.

And now, an absence
of all of these.
The eagles, proud and
wild, move on, transiently
stopping by the cottonwood.
Big Boy, the clumsy
one who walked into
our yard, is now indistinguishable
among the striped ones.
I never felt this in the city.
Each season
a chapter unto itself.
Each one has its
own name.
Each one a little different.

And I pine much easier,
for time is but a river
we go swimming in
and I can feel the
hastiness and greed
of a ticking clock as
it speeds on by with
every wave.

This summer
of stillness.
We look back on two years
already.
Two days?

6.11.16

AUTHOR'S NOTE: *"Time is but a river we go swimming in" is a line inspired by one of my favorites:*

"Time is but the stream I go a-fishing in. I drink at it; but while I drink I see the sandy bottom and detect how shallow it is. Its thin current slides away, but eternity remains."
—Henry David Thoreau, Walden

Dying Raccoon

One thing to behold,
a dead raccoon,
quite another
to watch one
dying.
The nature of death
is red,
an occurrence
enlightening and
demystifying.

No calm passing
to recollect his
yesteryears.
He lay there writhing,
with my girls in tears.

Sheriff says
"Welp, not much we kin do here.
He can't hardly walk—
you've got nothing to fear."

An hour or more
still clawing the dirt,
slower now
but I know it still hurts.
I struggle to come up
with a poison in my head.
How do I not know this—
how to help something be
dead?

There's no
peace in any of it.
It would only be right
to help him go.
More people arrive from home
hard to avoid this
macabre show.

A young fine gunslinger
arrives to save
the day,
pulls a rifle point-blank
and Mr. Poorsonofagun
is finally on his way.

But it's hard to fully erase
the space we all just shared.
Starving, gasping, clawing for breath
his words would have been,
"Good god, kill me already,
How is this fair?
I'm out in broad daylight,
I lie here at your feet,
crawling in circles on my knees,
everything has grown too weak.
I know not my home or
sky,
the pain sears my brain.
Have mercy and kill me now,
at this point I'd rather die."

6.15.16

My Fish

A fish swam close to the dock one day,
leapt with might onto the creaky boards,
detritus of life from its wake
rained on down, you mighty fish lord

silently
its rhythm
I noticed
worked the air
with force,
I poked it once
to snare some
attention
scales of slime
yet coarse

will you bother with me at all then?
you decided to travel all this way.
sacrificing the means to breathe
and now on this here dock you lay

I poke you
and hold you,
your eyes,
do they feel?
would you
rather be
a fish again,
forever
to face the
reel?

6.20.16

Wind

blue wind chimes
ringing
in my head
you shake the
space between the
rods
and my brain
begins to tremble
and bend
trees—
they reach to touch
the earth
then whip back in
fright
river
escapes on down to
Iowa
where the
weather is quiet
and
nice

6.20.16

How To Help Your Water

I hope this book has inspired you to look at the Mississippi in a different way, but most importantly, to realize that it's something worth protecting. Below are some suggestions you can do to help the Mississippi River and your local watershed. Try one on for size and see how it fits. This is in no way an exhaustive list and I believe you will discover your own creative way to see the sparkling glory of our river for all it is worth.

Dipping Your Toes In

- ❖ Buy a coffee mug and a water bottle and commit to reuse
- ❖ Keep leaves, grass clippings and fertilizer off the street
- ❖ Pick up pet waste
- ❖ Use a commercial car wash where the water is recycled
- ❖ Keep your vehicle tuned up and clean up spills if it leaks
- ❖ Use phosphorus-free soaps and cleaners in the house. Arm & Hammer is one of my favorites—check the Good Guide website to look up your products
- ❖ Wear organic materials in your clothing—microfiber is polluting the river
- ❖ Dispose of paints, stains, and oils at local recycling center instead of throwing them away

- ❖ Only apply salt when temperatures are above 15º F—use sand otherwise
- ❖ Want salt alternatives? Kitty litter, sawdust, or wood ashes (thanks Bob Vila!)
- ❖ Comply with catch-and-release rules when fishing
- ❖ Run through your sprinkler when you run it in the morning
- ❖ Do not buy products with plastic microbeads, especially soaps, toothpaste, and face cleaner (read the label!)
- ❖ Commit to reusable bags for shopping—recycle plastic bags, carry it in your tote, or choose paper! Trader Joes is great for reusables
- ❖ Go to the river! If it is your first time try a day trip to Lake Pepin for awe's sake
- ❖ Visit www.cleanwatermn.org for more ideas

Up to Your Knees

- ❖ Research your local watershed—for example, www.mnwatershed.org—to begin
- ❖ Attend a rain barrel workshop—it is likely your local watershed will host one
- ❖ Research native and sustainable gardening practices
- ❖ Ramp up your social media connections to include local conservation efforts
- ❖ Donate to any of the programs mentioned in this book
- ❖ Promote fishing and hunting with non-lead gear. Lead pollution in the water comes from lead tackle and ammunition fragments
- ❖ Research local energy rebate programs—in Minnesota, see Xcel Energy Rebate Programs

❖ Buy a flow restrictor for your faucet from a local hardware store

❖ Sign-up for a hands-on restoration volunteer shift—FMR or Great River Greening are good places to start

❖ Learn about the river by visiting locations like the Mill City Museum, Science Museum, or The National Eagle Center

❖ Visit Lake Itasca to see where it all began

❖ Learn about winter salt and sanding practices—www. pca.state.mn.us/water is a good place to start

❖ Read about the Mississippi River—subscribe to *Big River Magazine*, read local author Dennis Barker's *The River Road*, borrow a Mark Twain book from the library, nab a copy of the latest River Report at www.stateoftheriver.com, or follow the 1Mississippi Blog. The options are endless!

❖ Find Mississippi River art—Larsh Bristol Photography and following The Floating Neutrinos (www. floatingneutrinos.com) are good places to start

❖ Use the Mississippi Paddle Share program and kayak the river

❖ Bike the Mississippi River Trail—visit www.dot.state. mn.us/bike for a list of trails

❖ Request that your favorite local restaurants and bars have cigarette butt receptacles—cigarettes are a major pollutant to the river

Cannonball

❖ Sign relevant petitions and join frontline protesting— follow sites like Clean Water Action for campaigns

❖ Become a member or sponsor of a river non-profit like Friends of Pool 2, Friends of the Mississippi River, Friends of the Mines of Spain (Iowa), Living Lands & Waters, Great River Greening, or Mississippi Park Connection

❖ Adopt a storm drain through www.adopt-a-storm-drain. org or through the city of Minneapolis or Saint Paul

❖ Plan a family vacation with the river—the American Queen Steamboat Company is exciting, or rent your own!

❖ Apply for a stewardship grant through your local watershed district to install rain gardens, restore shoreline, or work with water use and permeable hardscapes

❖ Adopt a river mile through www.livinglandsandwaters.org

❖ Use the State of the River Teacher's Guide in your classroom

❖ Learn how the US Army Corps of Engineers is involved with the waterways, like they were with the Dakota Access Pipeline Project

❖ Interested in going to school for environmental studies? Apply for a scholarship through Red Wing Wildlife Refuge

❖ Research and join local land trusts, Audobons, and conservancies

❖ Download a lesson plan from H2O for Life and choose a partner school in a developing country

❖ Follow and support First Nations endeavors to protect the environment

❖ Link your love of local water to the global with The International Rivers list titled "20 Things You Can Do For Rivers and Rights"

Water is Life!

Resources

Audubon MN: mn.audubon.org

Big River Magazine List of Resources:
www.bigrivermagazine.com/bigriverlinks groups.html

Clean Water Action: www.cleanwateraction.org/

Clean Water MN: www.cleanwatermn.org

Ecel Energy Rebates:
www.xcelenergy.com/programs and rebates

Floating Neutrinos: www.floatingneutrinos.com/

Friends of Pool 2: www.friendsofpool2.org/

Friends of the Mines of Spain: www.minesofspain.org/friends/

Friends of the Mississippi River: fmr.org

Good Guide: www.goodguide.com

Great River Greening: www.greatrivergreening.org

Green Lands, Blue Waters: greenlandsbluewaters.net

H2O for Life: www.h2oforlifeschools.org

Living Lands & Waters: livinglandsandwaters.org

Minnesota Association of Watershed Disctrics Inc.:
www.mnwatershed.org

Minnesota Department of Transportation:
www.dot.state.mn.us/bike

Minnesota Pollution Control Agency: www.pca.state.mn.us

Mississippi Park Connection: parkconnection.org/

Mississippi River Network:
1mississippi.org/list-of-mrn-organizations/

River Life Partnership U of MN: riverlife.umn.edu

Standing Rock: standingrock.org

U.S. Dept. of Health & Human Services Product Database:
hpd.nlm.nih.gov/index.htm

About the Author

Cole W. Williams loves to write. She began writing stories and poetry as a young child and continues to explore the world through observation and verse. Williams currently resides in St. Paul, Minnesota.

For more tales about the river, science, and life on the Mississippi, visit https://www.colewwilliams.com.

Support local authors, support local bookstores, and build community!